Meetings That Make A Difference

100 tips for better meetings

Jonathan Frost

First Published in June 2015 by Discovery Coaching Limited

Edition 1

Cover Picture: Oberonsk

ISBN: 1517099978
ISBN-13: 978-1517099978

Also by Jonathan Frost

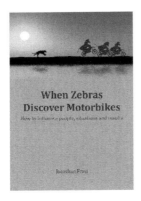

When Zebras Discover Motorbikes
How to influence people, situations and results

Life in the Serengeti changes significantly when the zebras discover motorbikes. The 'natural order' that the lions enjoy is changed. The 'zebra analogy' talks about change at work and draws your attention to the typical reactions that people have. This book has a practical approach and provides managers with a wide range of tips, hints and techniques to engage with and thrive on organisational change. It has an engaging 'coaching' approach that provokes you to think deeper, see things differently and do different things.

Jonathan Frost

About the Author

Jonathan Frost is the Founder and Managing Director of Discovery Coaching Limited; a successful Coaching Consultancy based in Edinburgh, Scotland. Working across Europe he has assisted hundreds of managers and directors over the last 17 years clocking up thousands of hours of experience in coaching delivery.

He has a unique ability to provoke thought, trigger discoveries and reinforce learning. His focus is on enabling people to discover practical tips, hints and techniques that are relevant to their everyday leadership life. Jonathan developed the coaching methodology known as 'Discovery Coaching' and this proven approach helps individuals to develop their leadership approach, maximise their performance and manage difficult situations. He is an inspirational coach who motivates leaders to excel.

Jonathan has extensive experience working with leaders at all levels in many different organisations; from small enterprises right through to large multinationals. This has included industries as diverse as retail, distribution, professional services, utilities, local government, defence and engineering.

If you would like to receive further tips, hints, techniques and offers from Jonathan, you can join his mailing list at www.discoverycoaching.com

CONTENTS

Jonathan Frost

1

DECIDE TO BE A 'MEETINGS' SUBJECT MATTER EXPERT

As a consultant and coach I have worked with many different organisations, in varied industries and in different countries. Almost without exception when the subject of 'meetings' is raised it is accompanied by groans, complaints and horror stories. People like to 'bash' meetings and there is always a willing audience who will share your pain and then tell you of theirs. If you are not careful this can give you the impression that most meetings are a waste of time and a mild form of abuse. This is not true and it never has been. Millions of business meetings occur throughout the world every day and if they were all like the stories that we hear, they simply would not take place.

We tend not to focus on the parts of our life in meetings when great discoveries were made, when light bulb moments were experienced or when there was an outbreak of consensus. We can miss that trigger point when the team gelled, became different and really started working together. We tend not to factor in the times when the organisational future was changed due to the presentation of a persuasive and compelling proposition. We might remember an intense disagreement during an interaction, but not the change in outlook or dynamics that resulted from that uncomfortable situation.

Meetings definitely matter.

They influence things at all levels within the organisation. Obviously they contribute to the creation of the vision, the strategy and the goals as key people get together to think and plan. It is meetings that enable these high level plans to filter through to groups and departments. They facilitate thinking and planning and in turn this has a significant impact on the allocation of scarce organisational resources. They are the platform that triggers and enables helpful discussion. Meetings convert debate and discovery into a fruitful and productive activity; this directly impacts the speed and quality of decision-making. Meetings are a major source of information, insight and communication. They represent an opportunity to convert data into meaning and situations into understood risks or opportunities.

Your meetings will have the effect of creating, transferring or dissipating energy. Energy is actually created as people gain clarity and are inspired into action. They begin to see 'what can be' and contribute their enthusiasm and engagement to the cause. This is then transferred to others when they go back to their own 'sphere of influence' and take the message with them.

Of course all of this can work in exactly the opposite direction; this becomes evident when the experience at meetings actually saps energy and enthusiasm. It happens if meetings are full of risks or 'blame storming'; it occurs when meetings are boring. When this happens all of the goodwill, energy and engagement actually dissipates; it is like a battery that just loses its charge.

It is important to remember that we 'frame' our reality. We note certain events and happenings and draw conclusions from them. In our minds we create a memorable picture and then put a frame around it thus capturing the image; this can create a consistent and unquestioned reality. I would like to suggest to you that there is great value in 'recalibrating' your reality in this area. Remove the frame and keep adding more pieces to the picture that you have. If you add in a whole bunch of helpful tips, hints and techniques to your meetings picture you will have a significant impact on those that you attend or plan for; this is true whether you are the leader, facilitator or participant.

Meetings will be a constant in your working world.

Whenever a number of people form a group and start to organise themselves to work together - meetings will be a required constant. It is necessary for these individuals to communicate and relate to each other; this is what will make the difference between individuals working independently or working as a team. They have no right to expect their outlooks, approaches and activities to simply align themselves. It is necessary for the group to create some common understanding, a common focus and a common set of objectives. Without meaningfully meeting together it is impossible to have the communication, collaboration and team working that an organisation strongly depends on. So my advice is to accept that meetings will be a 'constant' in your working world and decide to make them work for you as opposed to work against you.

This book contains a wide range of tips, hints and techniques that you can use to make meetings a powerful part of your working world. They are designed to enable you to influence their dynamics and make them relevant and interesting. These are occasions that you can use to influence the people in your 'sphere of influence', to influence the groups that you rely on and even to change organisational culture. Forget the negative stereotypes;

great meetings will motivate, empower and enable great performance from you and your team.

Decide to be a meetings 'subject matter expert'

This is the best way to create a new reality for you. Rise above the issues and take full advantage of all the opportunities that successful meetings can provide you. If you make such a decision, and see it as a binding commitment, it will indeed create a very different working world for you. You will have the insight to recognise helpful and unhelpful situations and have the expertise to respond and influence them. If you make such a decision you will actively look for ways to fulfil it and this will accelerate your learning and increase your influence in your organisation. Having profound influence through meetings can be your strength.

It is essential to recognise that for many of us our meetings are not 'internal' i.e. with our colleagues: they are also external with customers, suppliers, stakeholders and partners. The tips, hints and techniques that are provided in the following pages apply to all meetings because they represent general and foundational 'good practice'.

Thought Provokers

Are people trying to get into your meetings or to get out of them?
If you set out to have productive, interesting and relevant meetings then you will find that people are eager to attend and will give you priority in their diaries.

Are you an acknowledged expert at meeting facilitation?
If you are then you will have the eyes and ears of senior managers and you will be seen to be an important

cog in the organisation. You will be seen to be an enabler and a catalyst.

Consider the meetings that you engage in...do they create, transfer or dissipate energy?

Essentially this question asks you to think about whether the meetings that you lead or contribute to are helping or hindering success?

Can you think of any other activity your organisation engages in that impacts people, situations and results like meetings do?

You can extract a significant return on your investment of time, energy and focus from meetings.

Jonathan Frost

2

REDEFINE THE MEANING OF A MEETING

If you were asked to define the word 'meeting' – what would you say? Typically people talk in terms of two or more people getting together (by agreement) and discussing something. This is not wrong but it is not fully right either. If you redefine what it actually means you can adopt a richer and fuller understanding and this will provoke you to see more opportunities to gain from the meetings that you lead and attend; you can make them work harder for you.

Consider the list below of some comments that people have made about how they personally see meetings. They have come from different angles and perspectives however think about the benefits that you would gain if you added them all together; what impact would it have if everyone in your team adopted them? Think about the change in outlook and perspective if each individual saw things this way...

"Meetings are a way to influence my colleagues and be influenced by them"

"Meetings are a way to 'pool' our team's wide range of experience and knowledge"

"Meetings are a way we enrich each other's insight and experience"

"Meetings are our way to discover new outlooks, approaches and attitudes"

"Meetings provide us with a platform to share information. We talk to make sense of it and take decisions based on it"

"Meetings are actually an expression of our teamwork and collaboration"

"Meetings are our opportunity to provoke progress"

"Meetings are a great opportunity to influence people, situations and results"

If everybody understands these points and decides to be influenced by them it will create a groundswell of changed approaches and activities; this could make a significant difference to your organisation. The first point is all about being prepared to influence and be influenced. This approach of 'having a view' but being prepared to add to it and enrich it creates a powerful learning environment. It reinforces the value of 'richness' to the team in areas of thinking, discussion and debate. It also provokes cooperation and removes the 'competition' element of fighting to get your point heard or accepted.

The second comment recognises the value of combining or pooling the experience or insight that each participant brings to the table.

Imagine if five different people each had 20 pieces of a 100-piece jigsaw. Each of them holds one fifth, a significant piece of the puzzle, but ultimately without the others there is little use for their part. They might talk together at different times and trade pieces with each other. Perhaps one individual collects all the blue pieces (sky) whilst another collects the green pieces (grass) and yet another trades hers for the stone coloured shapes (building). They have certainly added value to their share of the picture that they own; they have interacted as individuals and benefitted from it. One has a clear picture of the sky, another has a picture of a rolling meadow whilst another seems to have an image of a stone built cottage. This is good progress, but it is not good enough!

It is only when they all meet together and 'pool' their insight and resources that the overall picture emerges together with its full meaning and clarity. This pooled insight creates new perspectives and dimensions and this adds even more value to the new overall picture. It forms a great platform for further discovery and engagement. A well-run meeting provides the structure for all of this to happen; it triggers interactions that provoke these benefits. This is how they can influence and impact every part of your working world.

The fifth comment talks about a 'platform' to share information. As mentioned in the previous chapter when people gather together they do need to structure themselves to be efficient and effective. This structure is needed to enable easy conversation and communication. This point refers to meetings providing that structure so that a) there is an opportunity to discuss and debate and b) everyone knows the rules how to do this productively. It is important to recognise the difference between something being formal compared to it being structured. Meetings do not need to be formal i.e. ceremonious, traditional or ritualistic; there is no need for them to be fixed and prescribed in their approach. There is however a need for them to be structured i.e. to have order, process and format. It is my experience that the difference between *formal* and *structured* is not widely appreciated and that many incorrectly see them to be the same thing. Structure may result from formality however that is not always the case and any assumption that it is should be validated.

The sixth statement talked about meetings actually being an expression of teamwork and collaboration. This resonates with me and it is supported by my observation of high performing teams. They need to meet because they need meaningful interaction to function. They need the structure to provoke helpful dynamics and the opportunity to challenge situations and approaches. The team needs a structured setting to discuss performance, develop plans and validate progress. There is a worrying trend to focus on how long people spend in meetings and to try and cut this down. Some organisations are proud to announce the 'time saved' by cutting back on meetings. I would be a lot more comfortable with this approach if it were all about the quality and outcome of meetings rather than the man-hours that they take up. An exchange of emails will seldom have the same richness and value as an exchange of points during a conversation. Beware of the triumph of efficiency over effectiveness. It might be more efficient to send a quick email...it might not be as effective as a quick chat.

Collating all of the eight comments into a coherent but short statement is a challenge that is well worth taking-up. You will find it very helpful to drive a new way of thinking about meetings in your organisation and depending on the requirements and situations of your working context a definition could be...

"We will see meetings as a useful activity to collaborate, share information, make decisions and help each other to excel"

If you are leading or facilitating a meeting it is wise

to engage the participants in recalibrating their expectations of it. You want them to see the opportunity of getting these benefits and to feel some responsibility for delivering them. If you make them aware of the requirement and engage them in the process then you will see different actions and behaviours emerge. Perhaps you could introduce the following checklist during your introduction and then re-visit it at the end.

'Ways of Working' checklist

Did our meeting today...

☐ Develop helpful outlooks and approaches?
☐ Stimulate wise actions?
☐ Pool our combined experience and knowledge?
☐ Enrich our insight and experience?
☐ Provoke engagement and teamwork?
☐ Trigger progress?
☐ Influence situations and results?

When you do discuss it at the end make sure that you are carrying out an exercise to identify ways to improve rather than a post-mortem on what was not done. The goal is to provoke progress rather than find fault. You might find it appropriate to just concentrate on a few points each week if the gap between what you are aiming for and what is currently happening is very wide.

Of course all of the above still applies even if you are not the leader of the meeting. You can still use the points to provoke thought and make suggestions. I would strongly recommend that you do so by asking questions driven by curiosity rather than the blunt 'pointing out' that something is not being done.

Consider the two examples below...

a) "Our approach to this is not helpful!"

b) *"What other approaches could we consider?"*

a) "We are not working as a team!"

b) *"How could we pool our ideas and experiences better?"*

Option a) will trigger defensiveness and possibly resentment. You may be right in your observations but being right is not enough; you need to be influential as well. Option b) will provoke thought and engage people in looking for better ways.

Thought Provokers

Do you see meetings as opportunities to influence or as a drain of your time, energy and 'will to live'?
If it is not the former then I strongly suggest that you take the content of this book very personally. Yes, it may be about saying no to meeting invites, but more probably it's about using meetings differently.

Consider the checklist above and use it to evaluate some of the meetings that you attend.
What does it tell you? Are there areas in which your meetings could be more influential and productive?

Does your organisation, department or team need to recalibrate their understanding of what a meeting can do?

3

SECURE THE 6 BENEFITS OF 'COLLECTIVE INFLUENCE'

This is an important concept and whilst you may not have heard of it before, it has been a powerful and consistent force shaping you and your whole organisation. Essentially a 'collective influence' is the overall effect that a number of individual influences (such as meetings) have when added together. It is the sum of the influences that take place and it becomes the invisible force that impacts behaviour, thinking and culture. By way of an example, in some organisations there is a very strong 'safety' focus and many interactions, discussions and meetings keep this topic central and relevant. There is a collective influence and everybody gets the message; they live by it and by so doing they actually reinforce it.

The interesting thing is that the 'collective influence' effect applies to all organisations, both large and small, and it does not need your awareness or your permission to have an effect. In essence what one individual or group does influences everyone else and so it becomes a 'default' way of working.

This can be explained using the 'inner dialogue' analogy. As an individual you have an inner dialogue i.e. you talk to yourself all the time. You are engaged in a running commentary of your thoughts, observations and conclusions. You talk to yourself (in your mind) chastising yourself for not achieving something or patting yourself on the back when you did succeed despite the challenges. You think about 'what if...?' questions as you plan for today, tomorrow and next week. You find yourself asking all sorts of questions to understand your working world and you continually think about and comment on the things that effect you. These inner conversations are important to you; they help you to make sense of the world; they are an opportunity to inspire and encourage yourself; they are a means of planning and evaluating; they are a means of exploring ideas and opportunities. They also form a very useful 'role playing' exercise as you prepare to interact with people and engage with your sphere of influence. This inner dialogue is a vital element of you. The sum of it reflects you and affects your choices of outlook, approach and activities. All this makes a difference to your typical and preferred 'ways of working'.

Organisations have an inner dialogue

Organisations also have an inner dialogue for all the same reasons. It is much more complex than that of an individual however the basic principles are the same. *In-house and external meetings are an integral part of the 'inner conversation' as members of the organisation discuss and explore issues.* They also debate things and decide on courses of action. The inner conversation continues as people make plans, explore options and create preferred ways of working. Through meetings the organisation broadcasts information; it promotes attitudes and approaches; it makes and publishes its decisions and it sets expectations about values. Meetings that take place strongly influence the behaviours of the individuals together with the meaning and purpose that they take on board. The sum of all these individual experiences creates a 'collective influence' that in turn creates an organisational culture or standard way of working.

All organisations develop a culture; a set of customs and adopted social behaviours. It results from the rich blend of different people and their varied outlooks, values and approaches. This accepted and reinforced 'norm' that we call an organisational culture is not accidental and neither is it random; it is the outcome of human interactions and obviously meetings are a large source of such interactions.

This is a significant reality that is commonly ignored; it presents both risks and opportunities. There is a real risk that this collective influence actually creates an unhelpful introspection. This means that the focus is internal; soul searching and self-observation become more prevalent than benchmarking and understanding the perspectives of others. I see this in organisations that have a reference point of 'what do we normally do?' In such a culture people who want to innovate and explore have to work very hard to try and persuade colleagues to look at what other businesses do – there is too much focus on what they themselves do. It's an unhelpful and disproportionate introspection.

Another risk is that meetings create or reinforce an inward focus that results in 'group think'. Everybody starts hearing the same message, with the same perspective and the same logic; in this situation everyone sees the same thing and they are comforted by the fact that all their colleagues see it that way as well. The group develops a well reinforced 'no brainer' perspective that is seldom challenged. This can unconsciously create a department or organisational firewall against new ideas, innovation or change. When this happens very small changes can be perceived as huge and brave simply because the starting point is so fixed in one position.

Of course there are also a good number of benefits that can result from a considered and planned 'collective influence'. These include...

1 The transfer of important values and priorities.

All organisations have values that drive their choices and activities. These are the principles, standards and codes that reflect the organisational 'personality'. They can be expressed in codes of behaviours, guidelines and statements; their purpose is to maintain what the key stakeholders find important. Cascading these throughout the organisation is quite challenging, especially for those with large numbers of people working within them. Meetings are an essential part of that communication and reinforcement. Messages about what is important can be communicated and reinforced in all meetings and people can learn about the values that the organisation holds to by their use in decision making, discussion and planning. When people see that the messages are consistent in different departments and at all levels, they readily adopt them. When people experience values rather than just hearing about them they become a much more relevant and powerful influence.

2 The creation of helpful coaching opportunities.

Activities during meetings reveal gaps in knowledge, skills and attitudes. These can be addressed through 'in-meeting coaching'. As soon as we see meetings as more than an exchange of information we will notice coaching opportunities as well as any disconnects. This is simply about helping participants to discover more helpful ways of seeing things and better ways to do things.

3 'Joined-up' thinking.

The frequent interactions, useful agendas, fruitful discussions and explained decision-making all help people to have a realistic and insightful perspective. They see the actual picture (not just the bigger picture) and this creates a very helpful 'joined-up' thinking. It means that everyone can be aligned even if they are not in the same department and do not work together. This is not a 'given' for any organisation and it is my experience that it is a very sought after position to be in.

4 Organisational insight and awareness.

'Organisational Awareness' is a very powerful state to be in. It means that there is a consciousness rather that simple communication; this provides a common realisation or a helpful and accurate grasp of things. The experience of your collective meetings can add together to create an awareness of people, situations, opportunities and threats. This can help you to plan for things wisely and be ahead of the game. The content, discussion and discovery of your collective meetings, across the organisation, can result in a helpful understanding of outlooks and perceptions. This is about massive knowledge and data being transferred into relevant meaning and understanding; this happens in well-run meetings.

5 Organisational focus and alignment.

Focus is all about concentrated attention. There is a limit to how singularly minded a large group of people can be and it takes considered effort to achieve it. Meetings with structure and wise planning are a great way to trigger, support and direct concentration. When a similar approach is taken across all departments and divisions you start to experience a helpful and common focus. This enables an alignment of purpose, focus and action. Rather than being a stifling or restrictive force on creativity or initiative, my experience is that it is quite liberating for those who thrive on working independently; it provides a context within which they can flourish.

6 Contagious energy and enthusiasm.

As mentioned earlier, when energised people interact with others, their energy is dampened, transferred or further ignited. Meetings are a good opportunity to transfer enthusiasm. They are able to transfer excitement and even create optimism. The way that they are planned, prepared for and facilitated will determine the effect that they have. The helpful energy that is created can infect others; this can spread throughout the whole organisation and even influence outside partners and suppliers.

So we see that the number and type of meetings that take place, their content and their approach greatly influences your organisation; they create a 'collective influence'. If you believe this to be logical and true then you will accept that meetings help to shape your organisation, your department and your working world. If you believe this to be true then it is imperative that you consciously and wisely shape the meetings!

Thought Provokers

How would you describe the collective influence/culture in your organisation? It certainly has one although I do recognise that it may be hard to put into words. If you decide to become conscious of this I am certain that you will see evidence of it.

Are you shaping the content, approach and success of meetings in your organisation? If it were easy everyone would be doing it. It is not easy and requires a leadership focus and approach. You need to see this as an opportunity – it is about 'what could be'.

How does your organisation evaluate the quality and productivity of meetings? Is it all about the specific content? Is it by 'ticking off' that certain meetings have taken place?

Appraisals and 1:1 meetings are a good indicator of how much your organisation recognises the impact of 'collective influence'? Are these seen as necessary 'routines' or highly valued interactions?

Jonathan Frost

4

ADOPT THE 7 PRACTICES OF A GOOD MEETING FACILITATOR

Are people trying to break into your meetings, or break out of them? The difference may well be in the way that you approach things. There are many different ways to describe the role of the 'meeting leader' including chair, convenor, leader or facilitator; of these I would strongly recommend that you embrace the role of facilitator. Whilst they all have special merits it is my view that the approach of facilitating an outcome rather than directing it usually has the best long-term results and enables the most people development. It is an engaging approach that wherever possible brings out the outcome from those assembled - it is a form of unobtrusive assistance that brings people into the discussion and provokes engagement. It can be said that the role of a facilitator is part leader, part navigator and part diplomat.

The **leader** element is obvious however it is not expressed in a directive way unless it is absolutely necessary. This is about setting the direction and focus and ensuring that everything that takes place actually helps the journey. The leadership element captures the role of *'custodian of the goals'* i.e. the person making sure that these remain the focus. Leadership can start taking place well before the actual meeting commences. The pre-work may involve collaborating with stakeholders; sounding people out or even a bit of negotiating. This is not a case of 'fixing' things it is more an approach to facilitate the best use of the resources and people present; it is about ensuring that the time spent is valuable and delivers what it needs to.

The **navigator** element of the role is all about understanding the 'destination' that the meeting is aiming to get to and seeing it in the context of the starting point. It recognises that there will probably not be a straight line between the two and that turns could be needed. Rerouting might be necessary when the group goes into conversational cul-de-sacs or starts going off on a tangent. The overview that the facilitator has helps him to understand when a departure from the expected route is helpful or unhelpful and is able to steer the group back onto an appropriate path. The navigator element captures the role of *'custodian of the journey'*. They have the map of the territory together with the intended route to take. The summary of the map might be a bullet point list known as the agenda. The navigator knows the goal behind each agenda point and ensures that the journey is appropriate to it. Good facilitators know that 'to talk about...' is seldom a productive approach and is usually a tactic rather than a goal (more of this in Chapter 7).

The **diplomat** element of the role is an essential one to keep everyone engaged; it is to ensure that helpful dynamics assist the meeting. This element captures the role of *'custodian of the dynamics'*. There is a need to 'recognise' seniority levels, positions, experience and personalities. A wise diplomat can smooth the waters of confrontation and correct people without it feeling like a rebuke. They look for points of commonality and then build on these to enable discussion and discovery.

In summary the role of the facilitator is part...

Leader   Custodian of the goals

Navigator   Custodian of the journey

Diplomat   Custodian of the dynamics

Facilitators Influence Dynamics

Whenever a group of people gather together they don't just pool their experience and insight, they also pool their personalities. They express their preferences, goals, priorities and problems. They have different outlooks and can prefer different approaches. Often they have different interaction styles and skills. Some will have a preference to listen and respond whilst others will feel a need to drive and dominate. Some will be consultative and want to gather the views and comments of others whilst others will simply want to impose their own views and convince everybody of them. It is intuitive for some participants to dive into the detail whilst others want to remain at a high altitude and take an overview. There will be some in the meeting who feel compelled to make quick decisions and 're-adjust' later if necessary; others will prefer a considered decision making process to get it right first time.

People often see their interaction style as an integral part of their success and therefore it becomes their preferred way of contributing to meetings. A skilled facilitator is needed to influence the dynamics so that the time together can be both efficient and effective. The dynamics of a meeting are all about the way that the individuals within it interact together. These interactions can be helpful or unhelpful and a good facilitator spots the impact and intervenes to make the most of the time and the people. Often, strong and wise leadership is required to manage difficult situations, unhelpful behaviours or even counter productive processes.

There are 7 indicators that a facilitator is doing a good job and they are described below...

1 They enable discussion and debate to flow.

This is not an easy thing to do. There is a common perception that the shortest route to any destination has to be the best route. This is not necessarily the case and can lead to a triumph of efficiency over effectiveness. Sometimes it is good for a meeting to 'helpfully ramble' so that a topic can be 'talked through' rather than just 'talked about'. Talking it through involves coming at the subject from many perspectives and allowing people to makes points, debate issues and come to conclusions. Just talking about the subject gives everybody an opportunity to talk but it is done so in a way that does not come to any conclusions or meet a goal.

There is obviously a big difference between 'helpful' and 'unhelpful' rambling. Often the difference is all about understanding the motives of the contributor. Some people feel that they 'have something to say'...and others feel that they 'have to say something'. Stop-Start meetings struggle to gain some momentum and without it people are not drawn in and engaged. You want conversation and contribution to be appropriately easy and to achieve this you might have to delay intervening.

2 They establish control and authority.

The very first step in this is to have a very good idea of what the meeting is trying to achieve so that you know what will be helpful or not to discuss. A good way of establishing authority is to send out a good agenda; this should state the overall goal of the meeting and have clear agenda points of what will be covered. It must state when the meeting is planned to start and finish; time allocations should be provided for each of the agenda points. This good practice primes people of what to expect and it steers them in the right direction in terms of preparation. Time allocations do give valuable insight into the depth of the subject to be covered because time given to a topic usually denotes a higher priority. One good way of establishing authority at the beginning of the meeting is to start off with a brief presentation by yourself stating the goals and informing them of the 'ground rules' that you want people to adhere to. Useful ground rules that can be established over time include...

Starting promptly – don't punish the efficient and reward the tardy by delaying the start of meetings. If you have someone who regularly disrespects others in this way take it up with them directly.

Reading materials in advance – gathering key people together is costly and logistically difficult. That opportunity should not be squandered simply updating people on things that they should have already read. Be insistent about the distribution of reading in advance and that gives people enough time to do so. Rather use the time to have fruitful discussion and make wise responses to the data.

Follow all topics closely – it is easy 'tune out' topics that do not have direct relevance to your role or which are uninteresting; fight this urge.

Allow points to be made – the minority of one can be right. It is essential that everyone recognises their responsibility to have courteous and helpful dynamics.

Make your point first...then provide all the explanation – quite often people build up a strong supporting argument and then deliver a flash of the blindingly obvious. Establish a practice of making points clearly and early. This can save time and protect attention spans.

Time keeping is everyone's job – ensure that everybody knows this. People cannot bring 50 slides for a 5-minute presentation. Attendees cannot expect to chase after all the red herrings they can spot but expect to finish on time.

3 **They maintain focus and attention.**

This is especially important when the meeting environment is not helpful; this might be because the room is too hot, lighting is inadequate or 'death by PowerPoint' is being inflicted. It could also be that the topic is important but not interesting. As facilitator you need to keep reminding people of why they are there, the significance of the goals and the benefits that can accrue. The idea is to give reasons to put aside the unhelpful environment and move on. It helps if you keep the group informed about the progress that they are making. The more active that you can get people to be the easier it is to stay engaged. You might need to create some 'what if...?' questions to get people thinking more about the topic and the goals. If you see that people are visibly tired and struggling to cope then announce a quick 5-minute break. If people start moving around and get some fresh air it often breaks a downward spiral of attention loss. If at all possible you want to intervene early in environmental issues, don't wait until it becomes unbearable because the worse it is the harder it is to recover.

People are motivated by progress and the more that you can summarise the successes that are happening the more motivated and engaged the team will be. If you promote the 'significance' attached to the meeting it also creates energy and involvement.

4 **They helpfully manage conflict and disagreement.**

It is important that areas of disagreement are not avoided. It is a sign of maturity in a team when it can disagree but still remain objective and focussed on the bigger picture and the meeting's objectives. As facilitator you can provide an opportunity for people to make their points and then give others time to rebut them and present a different proposition. The goal is not for one argument to win over the other; the goal is for everyone to feel that they have had an opportunity to contribute and influence and for the best outcome. Sometimes you have to intervene and state that a specific approach or behaviour is not appropriate and at other times you can let the group be self-managing. The principle is simple; when disagreement is *received* as personal rather than objective then it is necessary for the facilitator to intervene.

Contrary to popular opinion it is not necessary for the facilitator to be neutral; it could be that you also have strong views and want to raise them. A good facilitator does not however use the authority of their role to have their way, they rather allow the discussion or debate to proceed and only bring in their perspective later into the discussion. Remember that the role of the facilitator is not to 'negotiate a compromise' between two opposing views; the role is to enable the matter to be discussed thoroughly and for everyone to have their position heard. If a section of the meeting has been somewhat heated it would be wise to remind the group afterwards that it is healthy for them to disagree because they are all pursuing the same overall goal; it is right that people have to persuade others and be persuaded.

5 **They stimulate discussion and debate.**

When people gather together to address important issues it should not be assumed that everyone has the verbal dexterity to clearly say what they actually mean. For some it is a challenge to convert their thoughts into words and yet they could have a game-changing idea. It is important to allow them to make their full point. For some people they 'instinctively' feel that something is wrong but they do not have the skills to unpack the topic and discover what it is that is making them uncomfortable.

At other times a certain way forward may appear obvious or a 'no brainer' however again people recognise that it should be discussed in more detail. These are situations when the facilitator needs to stimulate some discussion and contribution. It might be about the need to ask some open type questions (who, what, why, when, how etc.) or it may be making a proposition or statement that people need to discuss. The question/phrase, "So all here are convinced that...?" can certainly elicit some discussion.

Another option is to provoke the group to think about it from other perspectives such as, "If we were in their position...would we be motivated or de-motivated by this?" Another way of stimulating discussion is to directly ask the quieter people in the meeting for their opinion or suggestions. If one person makes a statement you can ask others personally what their views are about it. Awkward silences are not helpful and often they mean that something is being 'unsaid' i.e. it is not being raised. It is the role of the facilitator to tease out the issues.

6 They identify and respond to unhelpful patterns.

In the next few pages I will be introducing some of the 'traps' that meetings can fall into. Skilled facilitators have an internal 'early warning system' for non-productive situations such as these and act to avoid them.

7 **They manage the decision making process.**

Quite often a meeting has been called for the purposes of getting a group of stakeholders together to make a decision. Sometimes this is a formal process and sometimes it is much more informal; it might be recognised during the meeting that a decision is required. The good facilitator recognises who the figures of responsibility and authority are within the group and ensures that it is not just a case of the most senior person announcing their decision. The reason for everyone being there is so that they influence the way things are viewed as well as the way that people feel about them. If it was simply a case of the most senior person deciding 'what will be', then there was no point in having the meeting in the first place! Using all the previous skills mentioned above the meeting is steered towards a decision point and then the facilitator facilitates a decision.

In the first instance it is wise to look for the common consensus. Are the group convinced one way or another? Simply ask them, "If I was to call for a decision right now...what would it be?" If there was broad agreement then a decision may have been made. Simply confirm that you are indeed asking for that decision.

The above option is fine if there is broad agreement however that is not always the case. There may be a few who do not agree and we should not simply assume that a majority is binding. You might want to follow it up with..."For those who did not choose that option, are you prepared to go with the majority or do you want to object to it and discuss the matter further?" This ensures that individuals have the opportunity to state that this would not be their preferred decision...or to keep the debate going. Sometimes it is wise to differentiate between those who feel really strongly about the issue from those who have a cursory interest. The matter may affect some more than others and so an informal 'weighting' system is wise. This might take the form of the 'directly involved' having more of a say than the 'observers'.

A wise facilitator will, in advance of the meeting, check out with the senior management what the process should be if there is no consensus. It may simply be that everybody should passionately and thought-provokingly express their view...after which the senior person will make a personal decision that is binding for all in the organisation.

Another option is to have a simple vote on option (a) or option (b). The option with the highest number of votes wins the day. I must urge caution about this approach.

In my view you often end up with a decision...but it has little commitment to back it up. Wherever possible the facilitator should use their personal diplomatic skills to drive towards a decision that all will agree to. Some may wholeheartedly agree and others may reluctantly agree – but it is an agreement and this is superior to a mathematical winning of one side over the other.

Thought Provokers

Which of the three facilitator's roles (Leader, Navigator, Diplomat) do you find easiest and most intuitive? This is important to you because you may well rely on it to the exclusion of others.

Which of the three roles is most needed in your organisation?

Have you been able to 'tune in' to the typical dynamics in your meetings? This is about being sensitive to what is influencing people to think and how to interact with others.

Of the 7 indicators that the facilitator is doing a good job...in which 3 do you excel?

- ☐ Discussion and debate flow
- ☐ Control and authority is helpfully established
- ☐ Focus and attention is maintained
- ☐ Conflict and disagreement is helpfully managed
- ☐ Discussion and debate is stimulated
- ☐ Unhelpful outlooks and behaviours are addressed
- ☐ Decision making is helpfully facilitated

What does it tell you about what you should be focussed on for your personal development?

Do you get the balance right? At times you need to stimulate discussion and debate and at times you need to prompt the group to make decisions. These could be seen as contradictory pursuits – what do you do to get the right balance?

5

APPLY THE 10 KEY SUCCESS FACTORS

A wise facilitator acts as a leader, navigator and diplomat to steer a group of people to achieve their meeting goals. They extract the collective insight, knowledge, wisdom and experience of the group and use it to meet the goals of the meeting. It is not necessary for the facilitator to be the most senior person in the meeting in fact it often helps if they are not. There must however be an understanding of and acceptance of the authority of the facilitator's role. Everyone must recognise this role and authority for the group to make the most of their time together.

There are at least 10 key elements of the role of a facilitator...

1 **Clarifying the Goals**

This is about knowing in advance the objectives and purposes of the meeting; it is about thoroughly understanding what the group needs to achieve. This enables the facilitator to drive, guide and reroute activities. It will be helpful for people to have both the micro and macro perspective in mind. It involves being mindful of the present and of the future.

2 **Controlling Proceedings**

This involves making sure that all of the required processes and practices are adhered to. It includes but is not limited to following the agenda, time keeping, discussions and disagreements. Wise facilitators set the pace of meetings to accommodate the richness of goals and the lack of time. The aim is to control the meeting and the opportunity that it represents, it is not about controlling people.

3 Steering focus and activity

It is very easy for a group to head off on a path that is interesting and stimulating but not related to the agenda. The role is to keep people focussed on the things that matter. This is about investing time not spending it.

4 Facilitating Discussion

This includes the use of open questions and thought provokers to start discussions. It also involves controlling when different people have their say, holding back others and bringing different people into the discussion at the most appropriate times.

5 Assisting Dynamics

This is about recognising the things that are assisting the helpful flow of dialogue and the things that hinder it. It certainly includes addressing controlling personalities, critical approaches and ensuring that the 'meeting joker' provides entertainment without being a distraction.

6 Triggering Collaboration

It can be necessary for someone to trigger discussion and collaboration between groups and factions within a meeting. This is definitely the role of the facilitator and it is a very effective way of making progress. The more that you are able to provoke cooperation, interaction and participation then the more successful the meeting will be.

7 **Involving Everyone**

It is easy to be a spectator within a meeting and simply to watch all the discussion and conversation take place around you. For some this is caused by a more introvert approach, for some it is a result of meeting dynamics and for others it happens because they don't feel involved. Whatever the reason the role of the facilitator is to involve them by asking questions, asking them to answer another person's question or simply asking for their view. Remember that the minority of one can be correct and profound.

8 **Confirming Progress**

This is especially important with long meetings. The role of the facilitator is to provide encouragement and context showing the group the value of the investment in time that they have made.

9 **Leading Decisions**

It is up to the facilitator to decide when lots of helpful discussion and dialogue has taken place and it is time to narrow the conversation down and steer it towards a decision. Without helpful leadership in this area it is easy for groups to just think of more and more examples and enter circular arguments without coming to a conclusion. This is especially prevalent in situations where a decision may be controversial or awkward.

10 **Capturing Actions**

Some meetings can go on for a long time and much is discussed and debated. It is essential that someone captures all of the decisions and action points that have been agreed and reflects this back to the group - this person is the facilitator. It does not mean that the facilitator is the person to physically capture the notes themselves but they have to make sure that it is happening. They make sure that the 'scribe' notes important things and every now and again gets them to summarise their notes 'so far'. This serves as a reminder of what has taken place but it also confirms and reinforces the focus.

Thought Provokers

Which 3 of the 10 success factors are a strength of yours? In which 3 are you most confident and successful? How could you validate your view?

- ☐ Clarifying the goals
- ☐ Controlling proceedings
- ☐ Steering focus and activity
- ☐ Facilitating discussion
- ☐ Assisting dynamics
- ☐ Triggering collaboration
- ☐ Involving everyone
- ☐ Confirming progress
- ☐ Leading decisions
- ☐ Capturing actions

Which are the two areas that you need to develop most?

6

KNOW WHAT INFLUENCES GROUP DYNAMICS

We know that human behaviour is never random and it follows therefore that behaviours expressed in meetings are not random either. There are often unconscious psychological forces at play and these interact to create meeting dynamics. People are individuals with different personalities, outlooks and approaches. When putting a group of individuals into a room with the instruction to interact, we have no right to expect this to be an easy, helpful or productive experience. When you think about it we have every right to expect this not to go so well. This section looks at some of the factors that influence group dynamics.

It is a necessary consideration because people will respond to and use the group dynamics in different ways. Some will wisely feed off the influences of others and find it motivating and useful; hopefully it will also be interesting. They may find that their creativity is stimulated and that they are empowered and enriched by the dynamics. Others may find themselves suffering the influences of other people and they find the process uncomfortable and even threatening. Challenge and confrontation may actually de-skill them as they are used to a very different interaction style. The knock-on effect of this situation is that they may start withdrawing from the interaction process and start avoiding eye contact, discussion and involvement. This is very unfortunate and it is definitely the role of the facilitator to ensure that the significant contribution that these people can make is taken full advantage of. As mentioned earlier, dynamics will certainly influence meetings however this might not be a helpful effect and therefore intervention is needed. The first step is to understand the drivers that influence things.

Everybody comes to a meeting with his or her own history and list of experiences. The series of events and occurrences that happened in somebody's past are welded together and they create a crude 'future predicting mechanism' by which they create expectations of what will happen. They bring to the meeting assumptions that have been generated according to what they have experienced in the past. The challenge is to change the locus of focus from the past (what has been) to the potential future (what could be). A large part of this is about the introduction and scene setting that you engage in at the beginning of the meeting. As you go through the agenda you can enthuse about the goals and provide comfort through your obvious authority, expertise and manner.

A big influence on dynamics is the risks and concerns that goals or the agenda may instil in people. A risk is a situation that might result in a negative outcome – it has not happened but it may well do so. It creates uncertainty, hesitation and even fear because we all find it natural to avoid risks if we can. If we cannot avoid them we become hyper alert to them and this can overwhelm our consciousness and take up our focus. In some cases this can be such a big thing that it is de-skilling and it is almost as if the risk has actually happened! People can, with good reason, be very risk averse and you need to be aware of this because it is going to influence their behaviour and therefore the group dynamics. It is important to think in advance about the 'risks' that people will be faced with as they engage with others so that they can be accommodated and minimised. Sometimes this will simply be about reassurance and at other times you might have to raise it during the introduction and state that it will be avoided.

If people are concerned that senior people are present; they don't want to make a poor impression and may decide to stay in the background – it is often helpful to get the senior person to confirm to the group that all thoughts, comments and approaches are welcome and that there is no risk.

Sometimes the very opposite of the above occurs and this is when some individuals are so keen to impress others that they keep monopolising the conversation, always answer questions first and are first to engage in debates. The risk to manage here is that others give up and simply do not bother to engage anymore. In the first instance you may find it helpful to keep pointing to others for comments, ask for the input from different people and make sure that the keen person only has an appropriate contribution. If this does not work then you may have to have a quiet word at one of the breaks. Say something along the lines of, "I really appreciate your engagement in the meeting. I am trying to get others to involve themselves to the same extent, could you help me to do this by giving others a chance to engage first on occasions?" If you do have such a conversation, make sure that you ask them for input pretty soon afterwards to communicate that you really do value their engagement. This keeps an involved person onside.

Power and the perceptions of it can have a significant effect on dynamics; it is an interesting dynamic and it comes from many different sources. For some in the meeting they may have the *'positional seniority'* and this delivers significant power over the rest. If they are wise and considered they will work hard not to provide undue influence as a result of their position because most times a group discovery is always better than an imposed solution. The facilitator will encourage those with seniority power to allow others to contribute first and ensure that they engage in discussion of the thoughts and concepts...not evaluation of the individual.

There is also a different form of this that takes place and we call it *'referred power'*. In most organisations, for example, the PA to the Managing Director wields a great deal of power and influence simply because of their closeness to the most senior person. Sometimes in your meeting you will have people who are not senior themselves but work directly for someone who is. As facilitator you may have to intervene and ask if they are there to represent themselves or their boss. You may have to remove this referred authority to make all things equal otherwise it unhelpfully changes the group dynamics. Sometimes such people are formally representing the view of a senior person and sometimes they are just being mischievous and using their referred power unadvisedly.

'Personality Power' is another strong influence on meeting dynamics. Some people just have the 'presence' or force of personality that demands and gets attention. They may be very passionate and persuasive about the things they talk about and they do not hold back in coming forward! Others have quite a combative interaction style and keep challenging things and people. They probably do this as a way of thinking things through but it often does not come across this way. People have learned to repeat whatever works for them and so if an individual has experienced the benefits of being quite aggressive, he or she will most likely want to

continue operating that way. It can be quite useful to say to such a person, "I am sure that you did not mean to come across so aggressively in that question, perhaps you could rephrase it to make the meaning clearer?"

Another common form of power that people use is *'expert power'*. They have some area of expertise or knowledge that places them above the others in certain situations and they can use this to position themselves as the overall authority for that matter. Knowing the most is not the same as seeing the most, or doing the most; so this type of power has to be seen in context. It is the role of the facilitator to judge the wise use of this expertise and when it is in fact becoming unhelpful. I have seen IT specialists have control over budgets and processes that have simply accrued because of their specialist knowledge about IT. It does not mean they are specialists in procurement practices for buying equipment, it does not mean that they are project management experts in implementing huge projects etc. The halo effect needs to be taken into account. This is when people are so impressed by one area of a person's capability that they automatically assume or transfer the same capability in other areas...even when there is no direct link or reason to justify the extended high evaluation.

The final source of power that I wanted to mention was *'reward power'*. This occurs when individuals are the custodians of budgets or other resources and this can mean that others have to treat them carefully, or at least think they do. This can happen where attendees from finance are present and the feeling is that they can authorise or withhold monies depending on how they are feeling. Of course in the overwhelmingly majority of times such people are professionals; they are not swayed easily and use their authority judiciously and in the interests of the organisation. It becomes interesting however when meeting participants change their behaviours or outlooks and project things to make points. When they act differently like this the facilitator needs to recognise it and intervene.

People's expectations for the meeting can greatly influence the dynamics of it and that is why it is important for the agenda to be clear and the goals to be transparent. Conversations with others, rumours and previous situations can prime people to have unhelpful expectations and the wise facilitator corrects this right at the beginning.

Thought Provokers

Do you have a well-prepared 'introduction' for meetings that you facilitate? Do you have a fluid and natural way to communicate your authority and the 'ground rules' that you apply?

Can you see the personality traits of different people and see how they are influencing dynamics? Are you able to tap into the dynamics and notice the helpful and unhelpful elements?

We noted 5 different types of power – do you need to adjust your 'blend of these ingredients?

Positional power

Referred power

Personality power

Expert power

Reward power

7

LET GOALS (NOT HABITS) SHAPE YOUR MEETINGS

It is very helpful to make goal setting a conscious and considered activity. This includes overall goals as well as individual 'agenda item' goals. If you don't do this you will find that habit, routine or strong personalities will take the lead in your meetings and they will be less focussed. In meeting management there are 6 compelling benefits that goals provide…these include to…

Create Focus

Trigger Decisions

Shape Thinking

Stimulate Activity

Provide a Benchmark

Prove Success

Goals do create focus. If you set out to achieve something, the very act of communicating this to yourself changes your behaviour. You start looking for and seeing opportunities to make it happen. You start noticing the things that you would only previously see; you find yourself more sensitive to and aware of all the different factors that could influence your success. This newly created focus is simply a 'concentrated attention' - it is when you filter out of your consciousness the things that are not relevant and you 'filter in' the things that might be relevant. We all do this all of the time.

Can you remember a time talking to someone who was fascinating; they were visually attractive and intellectually stimulating? What they were saying resonated deeply with you and you were discovering a whole new and helpful way of seeing the topic. In this case you probably had no awareness of anything else around you because all of your focus (concentrated attention) was on what this person was saying. This is what I mean by focus.

It is good to stimulate this during meetings because it helps people to 'link' together what they see, hear and experience to achieve the goal. It converts a group of people into a group of people with a common focus and that will always help with the dynamics.

There is obviously a risk that comes with this creation of focus through goals. It is that the goal might not be the most appropriate for the situation or that situations could have changed making the goal less relevant. It might be that circumstances and events require some agile thinking from the team and therefore the goal needs to be less specific and more general. The wise meeting facilitator has to understand this and to be aware whether the need is for a specific, narrowed down focus...or a wider, opened up focus. Is the need to converge or is the need to diverge? Another risk is that the group might become so focussed, so 'in the zone' that they develop 'group think'. This is when all of the people in the group develop a strong 'view' that is very similar to each other's. Each individual validates his or her own position based on the fact that everyone else seems to have the same view and the natural conclusion is that it 'must be right'. This gives the group great confidence and the issue begins to be seen as a 'no brainer'; 'group think' has emerged. A wise facilitator has to recognise this risk and use questions and thought provokers to stimulate wider discussion and different perspectives.

The 8-word rule

You may find it helpful to ask the group to confirm the goals of the whole meeting and the specific agenda points. If they are struggling to do this you may find it helpful to implement the 'goal statement thought-provoker'. Essentially this involves you asking individuals in the group to work individually...and write down the goal of each agenda point...*in under 8 words*. It has to be a coherent sentence which is concise and to the point. The value of this is that it forces them to just get to the point. To succeed in this they have to get rid of all the explanations and rambling; they have to say only that which is relevant. It is especially helpful to get them to read out their thinking; from this you can see the context of their working world; you can see what is important to them and you can compare these. This is a useful process to highlight and discuss the differences in purpose. You can use it to align everyone's thinking and integrate their ideas. For meetings that are regular occurrences you would not have to do this too often before the group engaged in self-learning and following that train of thought themselves.

Goals definitely trigger decisions in meetings and this is important because they are a gateway to many different activities and processes. Discussion, exploration and debate have to have a purpose; that purpose must be about more than being simply intellectually stimulating. Most times the organisation or group exists to achieve something and very often this is to pool their skills, knowledge and experience to be able to make wise decisions. As a facilitator you need to thoroughly understand the goals of the meeting so that you can identify when decision points present themselves i.e. those times where a decision would be wise or necessary. I have noted below some common examples of 'decision trigger points'.

The conversation goes quiet – everything has been said that needs to be said has been.

The conversation gets repetitive - more points and examples are being used however no new context or information is really emerging.

The discussion needs to diverge - perhaps it cannot do this without a decision on which is the better of the two routes to take. The group cannot take both of them; it is time for a decision.

There is a reasonable 'hard stop' i.e. the discussion cannot go on forever and so a decision is needed. The meeting has no more time to spend on this topic and the need to achieve the goal triggers a decision point.

This is a very important reason because many meetings that I have observed engage in an unconscious 'decision avoidance' activity. This is when the content triggers a decision and to avoid it the group decide they need more information, more time or more people to refer to. As a facilitator it can be quite useful to say in this situation, "I understand that you want to gather more information…if no such information was available…and you had to decide right now…what would your decision be?" This provokes a decision 'in principle' which many people find much easier. You can then follow-up with, "What does that new data have to say to significantly influence you to change that 'decision in principle' that you just made?" For the real decision-avoider they realise that there is no real difference that the data could make and they continue without delay.

Goals definitely shape thinking because of the focus that they provoke and the decisions that they trigger. It is important to note however that this 'shaping' of thinking extends well beyond the meeting itself. Earlier on you read about the impact of 'collective influence' and this is really the process of shaping thinking in practice. The goals become important and influential outside of meetings as well as inside and they become a natural part of work conversation; this creates a working context that is aligned to goals. If you don't have such a trigger to shape thinking then what would the influence be? Usually it means that the subject matter experts gain more power and influence; it also means that those with the strongest personalities and passion gain more power and influence. This is seldom a healthy situation for the organisation.

By shaping thinking and provoking focus, goals strongly impact the meeting; they trigger useful activity. You cannot make progress without taking action and the facilitator recognises when a stalemate has been reached and stimulates activity by asking questions or implementing activities. This is another benefit of the goals having a 'benchmark' role in that they enable you to gain a context for progress and a proof of success. This is how the wise facilitator uses their navigating skills to steer the meeting towards the goals and to keep everybody on track.

Thought Provokers

Do you have a reputation for creating a goal focus? Are you well known for keeping meetings 'on track' so that they are productive and efficient?

Can you cite good and recent examples of how you used a goal focus to trigger wise actions?

8

HAVE CLEAR AND CONSIDERED TACTICS

Having clear and achievable goals for the meeting is a good start to ensuring that time is efficiently and productively invested. You increase this 'return on investment' of your time even more if you have clear goals per agenda point as well. You can add even more benefit to the investment by considering the *tactics* that you are going to use. A tactic is simply the chosen way to achieve something.

Experience and talent has taught you to approach things in a certain way and follow patterns (tactics) as a means of accomplishing what you set out to do. Some of these activities will really help and others will not so it is important that you are flexible in your approach and open to change. If, when confronted by a dangerous situation, your tactic is to cover your eyes so that you cannot see it anymore - it is a tactic but not a wise one. If your tactic, in the same situation, is to run very fast - then it is much more helpful than the first one. If your tactic is to see danger well in advance then you have an even smarter approach. Of course it stands to reason that you have to apply a range of tactics in a meeting and it is the role of a facilitator to notice what is working and what is not and to introduce different tactics to maintain progress.

Quite often the reason that the group has been drawn into a meeting is because there is a need for the group to 'see' things more clearly or differently. It might be about changing a perception or providing better understanding. Alternatively the purpose might be to provoke people to feel differently about a topic or things in general. This could be about influencing values, priorities or attitudes. Obviously another reason for the meeting could be to get people to do things differently. This points to new tasks, different tasks or amended processes.

Whatever the reason, the meeting has been called to have an effect on the participants, very possibly so that they can have an effect on the organisation, or at least their part of it. The tactics involved in these areas of focus can be different and I would like to suggest that you consider the following types and apply them specifically to agenda points.

Meeting tactics...

Inform & Advise

Discuss & Explore

Debate & Evaluate

Decide & Close

Create & Innovate

Inspire & Energise

Warn & Caution

Inform & Advise

This tactic is best when you are using the agenda point to share information, insight and knowledge. It would probably involve the distribution of handouts with the data clearly presented and specific elements highlighted. It is important to put the participants into a 'receive and understand' mode when employing this type of tactic. You need to prime people to expect to receive information and that they will have the time to consider it and digest it. By 'priming' I mean to create an expectation of something or to prepare people for it. They need to know that there is an expectation on them to listen and carefully consider what is presented; at first the goal is to understand it not to react to it. It might well be that you do in fact want the group to respond to the data however it is always helpful to separate the *understand* phase from the *respond* to phase. The reason for this is that it stops people from jumping to conclusions, force-fitting their pre-prepared solutions or interrupting the learning of others.

It is often helpful to tell people to save their questions until a specific point in the presentation; you will be pleasantly surprised by how many are directly answered later on in the information, so it saves a lot of time and maintains a helpful focus. When you do ask questions it is useful to separate them into two stages. Firstly take questions that are about understanding and clarifying things. Only after that take questions that question the data, concept or conclusions. This helps everyone to discover things logically and at their own pace. It also is much more efficient and saves time.

When applying this as a tactic it makes good sense to prime people how to respond by...

Explaining WHAT will be covered

Explaining WHY it is relevant to cover it

Explaining WHAT people should do with the new insight or information

Discuss & Explore

This tactic is about using the agenda point to gain a deeper or richer insight of the subject. You might want to capture the views and perspectives of others. You want to understand them and engage different thought processes; you want to see how these integrate and overlap. You value the 'pooling' of experience and the subject matter expertise that the participants bring; you recognise the 'added value' that they can provide. It might be that you want to explore a range of options and in this sense exploring is a useful and appropriate word. By way of example if you explore the Amazon rain forest it would involve travelling through it and experiencing it. You would learn things from the journey and have a significantly greater understanding of it. To explore a place is to discover more about it, experience it and search out interesting elements of it. In the same way you can facilitate meetings so that people experience a greater understanding of the subject, the options, the imperatives and the ramifications. The organisation, through the discovery of the individuals, is able to wisely use the results of the exploration. When applying this as a tactic it is useful to…

Clarify why the discussion or exploration is taking place. What is the organisation looking to gain? Provide some context so that people can align their thinking in a helpful way. Purpose driven activity is always much more productive and interesting. When people understand the purpose behind a discussion it helps them to link helpful thoughts, observations and experiences.

Provide Parameters. Discussions can be very wide ranging and links to the original topic are very easy to make; the risk is that if things are too wide ranging they start skirting around issues. Without parameters the group might talk 'about' things rather than talking them 'through'. The difference between these two processes is in the outcome. When talking about something you may end up with a mass of data that really needs some other opportunity or meeting to collate and make sense of it. It is actually that 'making sense' which is the 'talking through' element – it starts extracting a meaning and message from the discussion. Talking about things is interesting; talking them through is productive.

Set some guidelines. There is a big difference between asking 'leading questions' and providing some guidelines. If the facilitator is asking questions that he or she knows the answer to and expects that answer then in reality this is a leading question; they are not helpful to the process of discovery and exploration. They don't really take you anywhere different or further forward. Guidelines give you an example to follow so that you can readily stay on the path. If we go back to the earlier analogy of the trip to the Amazon rain forest – you want a guide to help you navigate the route…but you want the discovery and experience to be yours.

Take the lead. As the facilitator of the meeting you need to recognise the difference between dialogue and a conversation that will help in achieving the goal. It is possible for interactions to be helpful, unhelpful and neutral. Basically only the helpful ones are worth spending time and energy on. You may have to open up new lines of discussion and you may have to close some down because they have exhausted their worth. Somebody has to do this in order to make best use of the restricted time available and that somebody is you!

Debate & Evaluate

This is about using the agenda point to present, challenge or defend things. It can also be about wisely weighing up options. It includes talking about things and helpfully challenging the perspectives or decisions of others. To ensure that it is not perceived as arguing, challenge the content without challenging the individual. This is an important capability for a group of people who aspire to be a good team; the ability to disagree in a constructive and helpful way is a sign of team maturity. This need not be a combative process but has to be an adversarial one i.e. ideas and positions are challenged and opposed. The evaluation element of this tactic may actually require some mechanisms such as developing a 'Points For' or 'Points Against' list or a voting procedure to understand the outcome of the evaluation. When applying this as a tactic it is useful to...

Clarify why the debate or evaluation is taking place. Again what is the organisation looking to gain and why is it relevant right now?

Set out the positions so far. You can save a lot of time by clarifying the starting point of any debate so that you are not starting from scratch every time. I often see many hours wasted in meetings when one side assumes that they know the position of another side and much debate ensues...when actually they are all in agreement about that point; it is other areas that require the discussion.

Intervene if there are unhelpful behaviours. It is understandable that people are passionate about their view and sometimes they get frustrated when they struggle to put in words exactly what they mean. It is also frustrating when people do not agree with you; a common response is to then say it louder (as if that makes a difference). Passion, frustration and poor manners can have a bad effect on dynamics and the facilitator must intervene. Their position is not to referee the dispute but to rather create an opportunity for persuasion to take place and for everyone to have their say. You might find it helpful to advise them in advance that you will intervene if appropriate. This primes them to expect it.

Decide & Close
If it is applicable to the goal, this involves bringing

the agenda point to a conclusion by triggering a decision point. If people want to talk more about it, it could be for a number of reasons; they genuinely may feel that they have not had the chance to make their point or they sense that the decision will go against them and so they want more time to try and throw in some compelling arguments. Again this might be a good time to use mechanisms such as voting. There are times however when there is a substantial and genuine disagreement. In this case you might want to include another option such as a 'not yet' choice. Instead of just having 'yes' or 'no' you could also have a 'maybe'. What this can do is clearly demonstrate that the group are not in a position to make a decision and this may be because they don't have the facts, don't have the authority or don't have the will to. If a decision is being avoided it is essential for everyone to be very clear why it is happening and the impact of it. There is also an inviolate rule that you must clarify what the next steps are to bring it to a conclusion; there is a difference between avoiding a decision and delaying it.

Create & Innovate

This is the approach to take when the group needs to think in different ways and come up with solutions, options or positions that are quite different from the 'norm' or the current situation. To create is to 'bring into existence'; to fabricate or make something that was not there before. Creating, building up new ideas or generating new and different options can add significant value to ways of working and in turn to results. It is this sort of thinking that enables 'competitive advantage' and clear differentiation from competitors. It is much easier for some than for others and the skilled meeting facilitator can recognise the difference and give opportunity to the creative thinkers to propose ideas and get 'airspace'.

Innovation is slightly different to creation in that the something exists and the innovator introduces a new element or develops a different approach. It takes the current way of working and identifies a whole new approach that is different (innovative). In meetings however they are almost synonyms of each other and when applying this as a tactic it is useful to...

Clarify why the innovation is required. Confirm the importance of the process with an emphasis on the benefits to be gained.

Provide 'What if...?' questions to provoke thought.

Provide 'thought-provokers' in advance. These can prime people to think wider, deeper or differently.

Present analogies. The group can test their thinking by comparing it to something similar.

Provide Case Studies. These can become a helpful focal point so that important principles, values and practices can be identified and applied to the organisation.

Set time guidelines. It is important that timescales are identified and managed. More time does not necessarily mean a better quality meeting; sometimes the sheer lack of time can provoke people to cut through all the 'froth and bubble' and get straight to being creative.

Inspire and Energise

Sometimes the people in organisations need to be inspired and excited; they need to be enthused and have their energy stimulated. A meeting can be a good environment to achieve this as long as those that are doing the presenting or discussion make a very clear and compelling contribution. People are seldom motivated by information alone and just presenting data will not do the job. It can also be said of course that people are seldom motivated by the enthusiasm and passion of others alone. When you add the two together however this can make a good impact and create long term benefits. When a logical, persuasive and compelling argument is supported by a passionate and engaged presentation then you can create an inspired and energised team. When engaged in this tactic it is good to…

Have substance i.e. real compelling benefits. It is the content that should inspire and enthuse.

Relate to people's hearts and minds. You want to present things that sound right and feel right.

Be honest. 'Spin' is seldom useful.

Remember that chasing gain is more motivating than avoiding pain! Putting people under pressure, fear or anxiety only provides short-term results.

Warn & Caution

There are times when one of the goals is to highlight to the meeting some risk that needs to be managed or a threat that needs to be taken into account. This might be about provoking a response or simply creating awareness. The role of the facilitator is to maintain an appropriate and considered approach and to ensure that such things are not taken too lightly; at the same time they should not be exaggerated. The balance is achieved by ensuring an objective approach that is processed focussed. By this I mean a thorough awareness of the processes, sequences of events or the 'paths' that actually create the risks. It is about understanding the context of the risk and the build-up factors that created it. It might be appropriate to look for ways of avoiding the threat and at other times it could be wiser to create contingency arrangements. When applying this as a tactic it is useful to…

Provide the facts that create the situation, risk or threat. It is best to create an objective baseline upon which people can build their concerns, and 'what if?' questions.

Explain the logic and the 'causal' effect. You want people to see the logical reasoning so that they can challenge it and understand it. This ensures that they feel 'in the know' and that they have a contribution to make. It is always helpful to identify and 'sense check' the causal link. Things can be linked without them being causal. Death by drowning may rise in number, directly proportional to the rise in sales of sunglasses. These two things have a link but it is not a causal link; the increase in sales of sunglasses is not causing people to drown! There is a common link: when it is hot and sunny people buy sunglasses. When it is hot and sunny more people go swimming. An unfortunate statistic is that the more people that go swimming the more people will drown. When you are giving the reasons for the risk or the threat make sure that the link between the facts are direct and relevant.

Know what you want to achieve. You don't just want to create fear, concern or de-motivation. Presumably you want increased awareness or a suitable 'plan B'. You might not know what this will look like (hence the meeting) but you know what an appropriate response is.

Thought Provokers

Do you consider in advance what would be the most appropriate tactic to achieve the agenda point goal? You will probably find that you use a number of the tactics i.e. you may start off with discussion and then bring it to a close. It is possible that you decide to warn and caution however after a full discussion and debate you tone it down greatly.

Which of the 7 tactics are you most comfortable with?

☐ Inform & Advise

☐ Discuss & Explore

☐ Debate & Evaluate

☐ Decide & Close

☐ Create & Innovate

☐ Inspire & Energise

☐ Warn & Caution

Do you default to your favourites?

Are you developing your capability with all of them?

9

AVOID THE 10 MEETING TRAPS

Whether a meeting goes well or not is more than just a matter of chance; it is a matter of design. It may be good design or poor design but it is not chance. You have no 'right' to expect group gatherings to be an enlightening, productive and interesting time unless you have invested some wisdom and effort to make it so. To make it interesting you have to identify issues of relevance and address them in an engaging way. There are a whole host or reasons why a meeting might not go well and I have outlined below a list of the traps that you will want to avoid.

No need to meet

Just because there is information to be shared or discussions to be engaged in does not mean that a meeting is the best activity to achieve it. It might be that simply issuing a thought provoker or a short survey would be a much more effective way to gather views. Updating people by email or newsletters may be a good way of sharing information rather than gathering people together. If you are going to call a meeting it is because you need the *interaction* of the attendees…if you don't need that interaction then you don't need people to get together.

It has become a habit

Meetings can be started in response to real and relevant issues but then the organisation gets into the habit of it. It simply becomes a dull routine that people see as a bit of a chore. They have long since forgotten the original purpose and someone scrabbles around at the last minute to put together an interesting agenda; but they don't quite succeed! The answer is definitely not to stop having the meeting; the answer is to recalibrate the goals, the focus and the mechanisms of gaining engagement. The only way to break the routine is by doing things differently.

One-way dissemination

If people think that the prime reason for meeting together is to be spoken at and downloaded to – then they will not find it useful or productive and they will not engage. Typically such a meeting can start well with everyone engaged and attentive and then it simply degenerates as minds wander and people feel that it is not a helpful experience. They then start checking emails and looking for work-type distractions. Remember that the value of the event is all predicated on the need for meaningful interaction. Interaction by its very definition requires a two-way experience and if it is not configured that way it will progressively lose its value.

Death-by-PowerPoint

We have all experienced the mind numbingly boring experience of an individual flashing a multitude of slides across your consciousness and then reading every single word of every single slide. This is not engaging, it is not polite and it is not acceptable performance. It is neither a genuine attempt at communication nor an attempt to stimulate interaction. This is especially true if a presentation is made up of a big number of slides listing reams of data. It's hard to follow and even harder to stay engaged. If you have a slide format that is replicated throughout the presentation so that the only difference is in the detail of the data – you have lost your audience! Your slides should give context and information in an interesting and visually attractive way. The development and advance of slideshow programmes has made it easier and easier to be adept at presenting in a way that goes beyond mere tabulated data. Use them to highlight main points and then talk through the ramifications or insight. If the slides can do their job independent of you then you are not needed. The remedy to this is to add value - enrich the learning and create a powerful experience.

The illusion of engagement

This is a point that has been referred to previously and it is all about talking around issues i.e. talking about them but really not talking them through. This can be a conscious tactic for some people because they can be comforted by the thought that things are being addressed. It's an illusion because nothing material can result from it and so people are not triggered to make difficult decisions or provoked into actions that are outwith their comfort zone. You usually have to address this at goal setting and agenda setting level.

The wrong attendees

There is nothing that can ruin the productivity of a meeting quite like having the wrong people attending. This could be a case of the 'subject matter experts' not being there so that technical issues cannot be helpfully addressed. It might mean that people are too senior for the topic and they simply get bored of the level of detail or approach so they disengage. It could also be because people are too junior and do not have the authority to represent their department's position or make decisions that are needed. This is something that a wise facilitator will be able to see in advance; they would approach the right people to rectify it.

If the technical people are not there you still have to do something, as it might not be appropriate to just send people away. You could engage the group in a discussion about what questions they would ask of the experts if they were there. You could discuss the issues and definitively determine which are 'real issues' and which are just 'symptoms' of the real issues.

If the people were too senior you could always change your approach and ask for their advice. You might use their seniority to link things to the bigger picture and get clarity on decision-making. You could even make it a discussion about delegation.

If your participants are too junior you could use the situation to gather useful insight and information. You could ask for their perspective of certain situations and clarify the key issues as they see them. They would find it helpful if the meeting crafted an approach that they would want to take with their line managers.

Unhelpful environment

This is a common problem and it should not be. It occurs when the meeting room is too small, there are not enough chairs, it is poorly ventilated or the chairs are very uncomfortable. These things make a significant difference to the overall effect because they hinder the attention and engagement of the attendees. It is hard to be creative or helpful when you are sleepy because it is too hot and you are not getting enough air. It is challenging to have a helpful interaction when you cannot really see the person well to whom you are talking and they cannot clearly see your expression or body language. If people are too far from the screen to see the small writing then they disengage and often start conversations with their neighbours. These things can be avoided at the planning stage however organisations often try to minimise costs and so they prefer to 'make do' and use the facilities available.

Other 'self-inflicted' problems include the setting of meetings at a time that is difficult for people simply because of a lack of thought about the travel plans of others. A meeting that starts at 10:30 may avoid a number of people travelling the day before and staying overnight in order to be there for a 09:00 start. Taking into account the meeting structure of other departments can be helpful as you don't want to set your meeting at a time when another department has their regular monthly meeting at which many of your proposed attendees must attend.

As a facilitator it is important that you are sensitive to these problems and do what you can to mitigate them. This might involve having extra breaks and asking those presenting to stand in a certain place. You might have to reconfigure the layout of the chairs or even request for fans to be used or doors to be left open. There might be an opportunity to reset the zoom level of the screen presentation. Remember that everybody is thinking, 'somebody should do something about this'...and they are correct; as facilitator that somebody is often you!

Rabbit holes

These are good for rabbits but not for conversations! The one common fact that we all know about rabbit holes is that they create a labyrinth of tunnels with many entrances and exits; also we know that there is not much light down in the tunnel. In business meetings a rabbit hole is when 'a topic is being discussed and it goes into a certain level of detail...that leads to a different level of detail...which leads to a different perspective...that leads to...' – you see where this is going. It is going anywhere and nowhere at the same time. It is the role of the facilitator to recognise that the conversation has departed from the realms of usefulness and needs to be brought back to reality.

Over selling

This is when an important and relevant point has been made...and then it is made again. Someone else contributes to support that point and provides a few examples. This reminds another participant of a time when it happened to them and they regale the meeting with their story. What you find is that a significant portion of your meeting is taken up only making one point...and even that has not been addressed! Don't confuse energetic conversation with useful conversation. As facilitator you need to recognise that this is happening, to confirm that the point has been well made and move the meeting on.

Mission creep

This can occur when the interaction and engagement of the event is working well and there is helpful and spirited interaction. After a period of time however some people with firm views or a personal agenda start to influence a wider and wider remit for the meeting. Subtly the meeting begins to change its goal. It changes its original intention and purpose and adopts a new or amended mission. At first this might look like the helpful application of initiative and enthusiasm however most times the group ends up overstepping their position, exceeding their authority or addressing issues that others are already engaged in. Mission creep is usually a triumph of enthusiasm over purpose and it is the role of the facilitator to highlight this and trigger a change.

Thought Provokers

Do you see any of the 'traps' taking place at your meetings? Is it a case of your focus and attention or is it down to things outwith your control?

The 10 traps…
- ☐ The need to meet is questionable
- ☐ It has simply become a habit
- ☐ It has become a one-way dissemination
- ☐ Death by PowerPoint is being committed
- ☐ There is the illusion of engagement
- ☐ Inappropriate attendees
- ☐ Unhelpful environment
- ☐ The meetings fall into rabbit holes
- ☐ Overselling takes place
- ☐ Mission creep

If you were asked to add to the trap list…what would you add?

Some say that 'mission creep' is the most important trap to avoid…would you agree?

10

USE THIS MEETINGS CHECKLIST

You will find it useful to undertake a structured approach to evaluating the efficiency and effectiveness of your meetings; the checklist below has been provided to assist with this. I would suggest that you might find it more helpful as a coaching tool rather than a specific metric for organisational evaluation. It is the sort of thing that you can run through after the main part of a meeting as the learning points are for everyone, not just the facilitator. This can even be the trigger for coaching colleagues on meeting preparation and participation.

Preparation

1   Had the agenda been read and absorbed by all participants prior to the meeting?

2   Was the reading material issued in good time before the meeting?

3   Did those who were presenting come prepared with visually attractive and intellectually stimulating slides or handouts?

4   Had the pre-issued materials been read and digested?

5   Was the meeting environment helpful with all the required resources (Slide projectors, screens etc.) being available?

6   Had meaningful goals been set and communicated for this meeting?

7   Had meaningful goals been set and communicated for each agenda item?

8   Was it clear what the tactics would be for addressing each agenda item?

Dynamics and Performance

9   Did the meeting pool the experience, insight and knowledge of those attending?

10   Did the group collaborate and work together?

11   Was the meeting a helpful platform to share information, make sense of it and make decisions from it?

12   Did the meeting generate enthusiasm, engagement and energy within the group?

13   Did the meeting provide an opportunity for all to contribute and present their view, suggestions and observations?

14   Did the dynamics enable discussion and debate to flourish?

15   Did the meeting facilitator helpfully and subtly maintain control?

16   Did the group maintain focus and attention?

17 Did the group make helpful decisions for the organisation?

18 Were the group interactions and dynamics professional, helpful and courteous?

19 Did the meeting fall into any 'traps' that hindered success?

20 Were actions, decisions and useful observations captured for distribution to all?

21 Were the meeting's goals achieved?

22 What worked well in this meeting?

23 What did not work so well in this meeting?

24 What will you do differently next time?

CONCLUSION

At the beginning of this book I noted that meetings have a huge influence on the organisation. They are the source of collaboration and interaction; they enable different people, with different roles, in different departments to work together and align their thoughts and activities. We noted that meetings can even create the 'internal dialogue' of an organisation and so they are influential on many levels. Over 100 significant tips, hints and techniques have been outlined in the ten chapters helping you to be a good leader, diplomat and navigator in terms of meeting leadership.

As you strive to become a meetings 'Subject Matter Expert' you will find yourself being consulted more in your organisation and you may get involved in more areas than your job title would suggest. This is because you will develop the ability to influence people and situations in an efficient way. This is a highly valued ability and your expertise will be noted. This will increase your exposure and reputation and with a bit of luck you may even be more liked! People will start seeing your role in meetings slightly differently and you will become a 'coach'; one who helps others to discover better ways of doing things. The 24-point checklist in Chapter 10 is a good coaching tool to help you in this.

Chapter 5 outlines the 10 key success factors for facilitating meetings and you would do well to see this as a personal checklist. Keep these 10 points to hand and objectively assess your performance according to them.

Perhaps the most important talent that you can nurture is your ability to sense, understand and influence group dynamics. If you can recognise the patterns of behaviour that are at play then you can influence them; cutting off the unhelpful and promoting the helpful. I am always surprised when people are not focussed on goals because they have such a powerful influence on us. Let goals shape your meetings not habits or routines; let goals shape your career not habits or routines.

I do hope that you enjoy your journey!

Jonathan Frost
www.discoverycoaching.com

Printed in Great Britain
by Amazon